Lace weight cotton crochet pieces make it easy to create custom jewelry designs in a wide range of styles. Endless thread colors and beading components offer irresistible choices. Basic jewelry finishing instructions are included.

LEISURE ARTS, INC. • Maumelle, Arkansas

Filigree Pendant

EASY

Approximate Finished Size: 1¾" (4.5 cm) (from point to point)

SHOPPING LIST

Thread (Lace Weight) LACE 0

[721 yards (659 meters) per ball**]**:

- ☐ 6 yards (5.5 meters)

Steel Crochet Hook

- ☐ Size 7 (1.65 mm)

Additional Supplies

- ☐ Tapestry needle
- ☐ 16" (40.5 cm) gold-tone necklace
- ☐ 10 mm gold-tone snap on bail
- ☐ ¾" (19 mm) button

GAUGE INFORMATION

Pendant (from point to point) = approximately 1¾" (4.5 cm)
Gauge is not of great importance; use any size steel crochet hook needed to achieve desired look.

PENDANT

Leaving a long end for sewing, ch 5; join with slip st to form a ring.

Rnd 1 (Right side)**:** Ch 3 (**counts as first dc**), (dc, ch 2, 2 dc) in ring, ch 1, ★ (2 dc, ch 2, 2 dc) in ring, ch 1; repeat from ★ 2 times **more**; join with slip st to first dc: 16 dc and 8 sps.

Rnd 2: Ch 1, hdc in same st as joining, ★ † (dc, ch 2, dc) in next ch-2 sp, skip next dc, hdc in next dc, ch 3, sc in next ch-1 sp, ch 3 †, hdc in next dc; repeat from ★ 2 times **more**, then repeat from † to † once; join with slip st to first hdc: 20 sts and 12 sps.

Rnd 3: Ch 1, hdc in same st as joining, ★ † (dc, ch 2, dc) in next ch-2 sp, skip next dc, hdc in next hdc, ch 3, sc in next 2 ch-3 sps †, ch 3, hdc in next hdc; repeat from ★ 2 times **more**, then repeat from † to † once, ch 1, hdc in first hdc to form last ch-3 sp: 24 sts and 12 sps.

Rnd 4: Ch 1, sc in last ch-3 sp made, (dc, ch 1, dc, ch 2, dc, ch 1, dc) in next ch-2 sp, sc in next ch-3 sp, ch 4, ★ sc in next ch-3 sp, (dc, ch 1, dc, ch 2, dc, ch 1, dc) in next ch-2 sp, sc in next ch-3 sp, ch 4; repeat from ★ 2 times **more**; join with slip st to first sc, finish off.

With long end, sew button to center of Pendant.

Attach snap on bail to any corner ch-2 sp and place on necklace.

Hibiscus Necklace

EASY +

Approximate Finished Size: 20" (51 cm) long

SHOPPING LIST

Thread (Lace Weight) LACE 0

[721 yards (660 meters) per ball]:

- ☐ 3 yards (2.5 meters)

Steel Crochet Hook

- ☐ Size 7 (1.65 mm)

Additional Supplies

- ☐ Starch and pins
- ☐ 16" (40.5 cm) silver-tone chain
- ☐ 7/8" (22 mm) silver-tone flower pendant
- ☐ 8 mm silver-tone lobster clasp
- ☐ 8 mm silver-tone round jump ring
- ☐ 5 mm silver-tone round jump ring
- ☐ 3 mm silver-tone oval jump rings - 4
- ☐ Chain-nose pliers - 2 pair
- ☐ Wire cutters

GAUGE INFORMATION

Motif = approximately 2¼" (5.75 cm) across each side edge

Gauge is not of great importance; use any size steel crochet hook needed to achieve desired look.

STITCH GUIDE

TREBLE CROCHET ***(abbreviated tr)***

YO twice, insert hook in st indicated, YO and pull up a loop (4 loops on hook), (YO and draw through 2 loops on hook) 3 times.

MOTIF

Ch 38, sc in second ch from hook and in next ch, hdc in next ch, dc in next 14 chs, tr in next ch, (2 tr, ch 2, 2 tr) in next ch, tr in next ch, dc in next 14 chs, hdc in next ch, sc in last 2 chs: finish off: 40 sts and one ch-2 sp.

FINISHING

See Finishing, pages 30 and 31.

Lightly starch Motif and pin in a V shape; allow to dry completely.

Cut chain into two 8" (20.5 cm) lengths.

Using chain-nose pliers, open a 3 mm oval jump ring. Insert jump ring through end of one length of chain and through loop on lobster claw clasp and close ring with pliers.

Open a 3 mm oval jump ring and insert it through end of remaining length of chain and through 8 mm jump ring and close ring.

Open 5 mm round jump ring and insert it though ch-2 sp on Motif and through loop of pendant and close ring.

Open a 3 mm oval jump ring and insert it around last sc on one side of Motif and through end of one length of chain and close ring.

Repeat with remaining 3 mm oval jump ring and length of chain.

All Keyed Up Necklace

EASY

Approximate Finished Size: 25" (63.5 cm) long (including Tassel)

SHOPPING LIST

Thread (Lace Weight) LACE 0

[721 yards (660 meters) per ball**]**:
- ☐ 6 yards (5.5 meters)

Steel Crochet Hook

- ☐ Size 7 (1.65 mm)

Additional Supplies

- ☐ Silver-tone toggle clasp
- ☐ Silver-tone 8 mm jump ring
- ☐ Silver-tone charms - 5

GAUGE INFORMATION

Gauge is not of great importance; use any size steel crochet hook needed to achieve the desired look.

NECKLACE

Join thread with slip st in loop at end of one half of toggle clasp, work a 22" (56 cm) chain; slip st in loop at end of remaining half of toggle clasp, work a 22" (56 cm) chain; slip st in loop on end of same half of toggle clasp as first slip st; finish off.

TASSEL

First Charm: Join thread with slip st around jump ring; ch 18, slip st in loop on first charm; finish off.

Second Charm: Join thread with slip st around jump ring; ch 13, slip st in loop on second charm; finish off.

Third Charm: Join thread with slip st around jump ring; ch 11, slip st in loop on third charm; finish off.

Fourth Charm: Join thread with slip st around jump ring; ch 9, slip st in loop on fourth charm; finish off.

Fifth Charm: Join thread with slip st around jump ring; ch 3, slip st in loop on fifth charm; finish off.

Slide Tassel's jump ring onto chain over bar end of toggle.

Olive Earrings

EASY

Approximate Finished Size: 1¾" (4.5 cm) long (excluding ear wires)

SHOPPING LIST

Thread (Lace Weight) LACE 0

[350 yards (320 meters) per ball]:

- ☐ 4 yards (3.5 meters)

Steel Crochet Hook

- ☐ Size 7 (1.65 mm)

Additional Supplies

- ☐ 2" (5 cm) brass head pins - 2
- ☐ Brass fishhook ear wire - 2
- ☐ 6 mm stone beads - 2
- ☐ Round-nose pliers - 1 pair
- ☐ Chain-nose pliers - 2 pair
- ☐ Wire cutters

GAUGE INFORMATION

Each Motif = approximately 1¼" long x ¾" wide (3.25 cm x 19 mm)

Gauge is not of great importance; use any size steel crochet hook needed to achieve desired look.

STITCH GUIDE

TREBLE CROCHET ***(abbreviated tr)***

YO twice, insert hook in st indicated, YO and pull up a loop (4 loops on hook), (YO and draw through 2 loops on hook) 3 times.

TREBLE CROCHET 2 TOGETHER ***(abbreviated tr2tog)***

(uses next 2 sts)

★ YO twice, insert hook in **next** tr, YO and pull up a loop, (YO and draw through 2 loops on hook) twice; repeat from ★ once **more**, YO and draw through all 3 loops on hook **(counts as one tr)**.

MOTIF (Make 2)

Row 1: Ch 3, work 3 hdc in third ch from hook: 3 hdc.

Row 2: Ch 4 **(counts as first tr)**, turn; (tr, ch 3, tr) in next hdc, tr in last hdc: 4 tr.

Row 3: [Ch 3, turn; tr in next tr **(counts as first tr2tog)]**, skip next ch-3 sp, tr2tog: 2 tr.

Edging Rnd (Right side)**:** Ch 1, turn; sc in first tr, 2 sc in last tr; working in ends of rows, work 4 sc in same row, sc in top of next tr, 4 sc in same row, sc in top of next hdc and in end of same row; working in free loop of beginning ch ***(Fig. 2, page 29)***, (2 sc, ch 1, 2 sc) in ch; working in ends of rows, sc in first row and in top of same hdc, 4 sc in next row and in top of same tr, 4 sc in last row, sc in same st as first sc; join with slip st to first sc: 30 sc and one ch-1 sp.

Loop: Slip st in next sc, ch 3, slip st in next sc; finish off.

FINISHING

See Finishing, pages 30 and 31.

Make a bead drop. Using chain-nose pliers, open loop.

Insert loop through ch-1 sp at bottom of one Motif and close loop with pliers.

Open loop on one ear wire, insert loop through ch-3 sp at top of same Motif and close loop.

Repeat for second Earring.

Ring Time Necklace & Earrings Set

EASY +

Approximate Finished Sizes: Necklace: 32" (81.5 cm) long
Earrings: 2" (5 cm) long (excluding ear wires)

SHOPPING LIST

Thread (Lace Weight) LACE 0
[122 yards (111.5 meters) per ball]:
- ☐ 20 yards (18.5 meters)

Steel Crochet Hook
- ☐ Size 7 (1.65 mm)

Additional Supplies
- ☐ Lever-back silver-tone ear wires - 2
- ☐ 1" (2.5 cm) silver-tone hammered metal rings - 9
- ☐ Chain-nose pliers - 2 pair

GAUGE INFORMATION

Gauge is not of great importance; use any size steel crochet hook needed to achieve desired look.

STITCH GUIDE

TREBLE CROCHET ***(abbreviated tr)***
YO twice, insert hook in st indicated, YO and pull up a loop (4 loops on hook), (YO and draw through 2 loops on hook) 3 times.

NECKLACE

First Side: Join thread with sc in first metal ring ***(see Joining With Sc, page 29)***; 11 sc in same ring, ch 38, (12 sc in next metal ring, ch 38) 6 times; being careful **not** to twist, join with slip st to first sc, finish off: 7 ch-38 loops.

Second Side: Join thread with sc in opposite side of first ring; 11 sc in same ring, ch 15, 5 dc in next ch-38 loop, ch 15, ★ 12 sc in next ring, ch 15, 5 dc in next ch-38 loop, ch 15; repeat from ★ around; join with slip st to first sc, finish off.

EARRING (Make 2)

See Finishing, pages 30 and 31.

Row 1: Join thread with sc in a metal ring; 11 sc in same ring: 12 sc.

Row 2: Ch 4, turn; tr in fourth ch from hook, ch 4, tr in fourth ch from hook, ch 6, skip first 4 chs from hook, slip st in next 2 chs **(top loop made)**, (ch 4, tr in fourth ch from hook) twice, skip first 11 sc; join with slip st to last sc, finish off.

Using chain-nose pliers, open loop on ear wire. Insert loop into Earring top loop and close loop with pliers.

Flower Brooch

EASY +

Approximate Finished Size: 2" (5 cm) diameter

SHOPPING LIST

Thread (Lace Weight) LACE 0

[350 yards (320 meters) per ball]:

- ☐ White - 15 yards (13.5 meters)
- ☐ Cream - small amount

Steel Crochet Hook

- ☐ Size 7 (1.65 mm)

Additional Supplies

- ☐ Flexible wire beading needle
- ☐ 1" (2.5 cm) pin back or barrette
- ☐ 4 mm stone beads - 7

GAUGE INFORMATION

Gauge is not of great importance; use any size steel crochet hook needed to achieve desired look.

STITCH GUIDE

TREBLE CROCHET *(abbreviated tr)*

YO twice, insert hook in st or sp indicated, YO and pull up a loop (4 loops on hook), (YO and draw through 2 loops on hook) 3 times.

DOUBLE TREBLE CROCHET *(abbreviated dtr)*

YO 3 times, insert hook in sp indicated, YO and pull up a loop (5 loops on hook), (YO and draw through 2 loops on hook) 4 times.

PICOT

Ch 2, slip st in second ch from hook.

FLOWER

OUTER PETALS

With White, ch 8; join with slip st to form a ring.

Rnd 1: (Ch 12, slip st in ring) 6 times: 6 loops.

Rnd 2 (Right side)**:** Ch 1, (sc, hdc, dc, 5 tr, 3 dtr, 5 tr, dc, hdc, sc) in first loop and in each loop around; join with slip st to first sc, finish off: 114 sts.

Note: Loop a short piece of thread around any stitch to mark Rnd 2 as **right** side.

Rnd 3: With **right** side facing, skip first sc and join Cream with sc in next hdc ***(see Joining With Sc, page 29)***; sc in next 6 sts, hdc in next dtr, 3 hdc in next dtr, hdc in next dtr, sc in next 7 sts, skip next 2 sc, ★ sc in next 7 sts, hdc in next dtr, 3 hdc in next dtr, hdc in next dtr, sc in next 7 sts, skip next 2 sc; repeat from ★ around; join with slip st to first sc, finish off.

CENTER

Rnd 1 (Right side)**:** With White, leaving a long end for sewing, and using an adjustable ring ***(Figs. 1a-d, page 29)***, ch 2 **(does not count as a st)**, work 12 dc in ring; join with slip st to first dc.

Note: Mark Rnd 1 as **right** side.

Rnd 2: Ch 2, (dc, tr) in same st as joining, work Picot, (tr, dc, ch 2, slip st) in next dc, ★ (slip st, ch 2, dc, tr) in next dc, work Picot, (tr, dc, ch 2, slip st) in next dc; repeat from ★ around; join with slip st to joining slip st, finish off: 6 petals.

FINISHING

With **right** sides of both pieces facing and using long end, sew Center to Outer Petals, do **not** cut thread. Using same end, sew beads to Center, then sew pin back or barrette to **wrong** side.

Choker & Earrings Set

EASY +

Finished Sizes: Choker: 1½" wide x 13½" long (4 cm x 34.5 cm)
Earrings: ¾" (19 mm) long (excluding ear wire and bead drop)

SHOPPING LIST

Thread (Lace Weight) LACE 0

[306 yards (280 meters) per ball]:

- ☐ 1 ball

Steel Crochet Hook

- ☐ Size 7 (1.65 mm)
  or size needed for gauge

Additional Supplies

- ☐ 2" (5 cm) silver-tone head pins - 8
- ☐ Lever-back silver-tone ear wire - 2
- ☐ 6 mm round stone beads - 8
- ☐ ¼" (7 mm) pearl button
- ☐ Round-nose pliers - 1 pair
- ☐ Chain-nose pliers - 2 pair
- ☐ Wire cutters

GAUGE INFORMATION

9 dc = 1" (2.5 cm)

Gauge Swatch: 1" (2.5 cm) square

Ch 11.

Row 1: Dc in fourth ch from hook and in each ch across **(3 skipped chs count as first dc)**: 9 dc.

Rows 2-4: Ch 3 **(counts as first dc)**, turn; dc in next dc and in each dc across.

Finish off.

STITCH GUIDE

TREBLE CROCHET ***(abbreviated tr)***

YO twice, insert hook in sp indicated, YO and pull up a loop (4 loops on hook), (YO and draw through 2 loops on hook) 3 times.

PICOT

Ch 2, slip st in second ch from hook.

CHOKER

Ch 123.

Row 1 (Right side)**:** Dc in fourth ch from hook and in each ch across **(3 skipped chs count as first dc)**: 121 dc.

Note: Loop a short piece of thread around any stitch to mark Row 1 as **right** side.

Row 2: Ch 1, turn; sc in first dc, ★ ch 3, skip next 2 dc, sc in next dc; repeat from ★ across: 40 ch-3 sps.

Row 3: Ch 3 **(does not count as a st)**, turn; 4 tr in first ch-3 sp and in each ch-3 sp across: 160 tr.

Row 4: Ch 3, turn; skip first 3 tr, slip st in next 2 tr, ch 3, ★ skip next 2 tr, slip st in next 2 tr, ch 3; repeat from ★ across to last 3 tr, skip next 2 tr, slip st in last tr: 40 ch-3 sps.

Row 5: Ch 2 **(does not count as a st)**, turn; (dc, ch 3, dc) in first ch-3 sp and in each ch-3 sp across.

Row 6: Ch 1, turn; (sc, hdc, dc, tr) in first ch-3 sp, ch 2, (tr, dc, hdc, sc) in next ch-3 sp, ★ (sc, hdc, dc, tr) in next ch-3 sp, ch 2, (tr, dc, hdc, sc) in next ch-3 sp; repeat from ★ across: 20 ch-2 sps.

Row 7: Ch 1, turn; skip first sc, sc in next 3 sts, (hdc, ch 3, hdc) in next ch-2 sp, sc in next 3 sts, ★ work Picot, skip next 2 sc, sc in next 3 sts, (hdc, ch 3, hdc) in next ch-2 sp, sc in next 3 sts; repeat from ★ across to last sc, leave last sc unworked, do **not** finish off.

Trim and Button Loop: Ch 3; working in ends of rows, (slip st in next row, ch 3) twice, skip next row, slip st in next row, ch 7 (button loop), slip st in last row; finish off.

EARRING (Make 2)

Row 1: Ch 7, dc in seventh ch from hook: one sp.

Row 2 (Right side)**:** Ch 1, turn; (sc, dc, tr, ch 2, tr, dc, sc) in sp: 6 sts and one ch-2 sp.

Note: Mark Row 2 as **right** side.

Edging: Ch 1, do **not** turn; 7 sc in sp on Row 1; sc in next 3 sts on Row 2, (sc, ch 3, sc) in next ch-2 sp, sc in last 3 sts; join with slip st to first sc, finish off.

FINISHING

See Finishing, pages 30 and 31.

CHOKER

Make 6 bead drops. Using chain-nose pliers, open loops.

Attach one bead drop to each of center 6 ch-3 sps on Row 7, closing each loop with chain-nose pliers.

Sew button to **right** side of Row 1 opposite Button Loop.

EARRINGS

Make 2 bead drops in same manner as Choker, attaching loop to ch-3 sp on Edging.

Open loop on ear wire with chain-nose pliers and attach to center sc of 7-sc group on Edging.

Star Flower Earrings

EASY +

Approximate Finished Sizes:

Version A - 1¼" long x 1½" wide (3 cm x 4 cm) **Version B** - 1" long x ¾" wide (2.5 cm x 19 mm) (excluding ear wires)

SHOPPING LIST

Thread (Lace Weight)

LACE 0

Version A

[350 yards (320 meters) per ball**]**:

- ☐ Green - 6 yards (5.5 meters)

Version B

[721 yards (660 meters) per ball**]**:

- ☐ Red - 2 yards (2 meters)

Steel Crochet Hook

- ☐ Size 7 (1.65 mm)

Additional Supplies

- ☐ Flexible wire beading needle
- ☐ Chain-nose pliers - 2 pair

Version A

- ☐ 3 mm pastel glass beads - 6
- ☐ 1¼" (3 cm) pewter-tone chandelier earring finding - 2
- ☐ Pewter-tone fishhook ear wire - 2

Version B

- ☐ 3 mm metallic glass beads - 6
- ☐ ¾" (19 mm) copper-tone chandelier earring finding - 2
- ☐ Copper-tone lever-back ear wire - 2

GAUGE INFORMATION

Each Flower = approximately ¾" (19 mm) diameter

Gauge is not of great importance; use any size steel crochet hook needed to achieve desired look.

FLOWER

(Make 6 for Version A or 2 for Version B)

Rnd 1 (Right side)**:** Using an adjustable ring ***(Figs. 1a-d, page 29)***, ★ ch 2, dc in ring, ch 2, slip st in top of dc just made, ch 2, slip st in ring; repeat from ★ 4 times **more**; finish off, leaving a long end for sewing.

FINISHING

See Finishing, pages 30 and 31.

Using photo as a guide for placement and long ends, sew Flowers to chandelier findings, working through bottom loops of finding, do **not** cut thread. Using same end, sew beads to Flowers.

Using chain-nose pliers, open loop on ear wire. Attach ear wire to top of chandelier finding and close loop.

Ruffled Cuff Bracelet

EASY +

Finished Size: 2½" wide x 6¾" long (6.5 cm x 17 cm)

SHOPPING LIST

Thread (Lace Weight)

[350 yards (320 meters) per ball]:

- ☐ 1 ball

Steel Crochet Hook

- ☐ Size 7 (1.65 mm)
  or size needed for gauge

Additional Supplies

- ☐ Tapestry needle
- ☐ ½" (12 mm) buttons - 3

GAUGE INFORMATION

In Body pattern,
15 sts = $1^5/_8$" (4 cm);
12 rows = 2" (5 cm)

Gauge Swatch: $1^5/_8$" wide x 2" high (4 cm x 5 cm)

Work same as Body for 12 rows: 15 sts.

STITCH GUIDE

TREBLE CROCHET ***(abbreviated tr)***

YO twice, insert hook in sp indicated, YO and pull up a loop (4 loops on hook), (YO and draw through 2 loops on hook) 3 times.

FRONT POST DOUBLE CROCHET ***(abbreviated FPdc)***

YO, insert hook from **front** to **back** around post of st indicated ***(Fig. 3, page 29)***, YO and pull up a loop (3 loops on hook), (YO and draw through 2 loops on hook) twice.

BACK POST DOUBLE CROCHET ***(abbreviated BPdc)***

YO, insert hook from **back** to **front** around post of st indicated ***(Fig. 3, page 29)***, YO and pull up a loop (3 loops on hook), (YO and draw through 2 loops on hook) twice.

PICOT

Ch 3, slip st in third ch from hook.

BODY

Ch 16.

Row 1: Hdc in second ch from hook and in each ch across: 15 hdc.

Row 2 (Right side)**:** Ch 1, turn; hdc in first hdc, work FPdc around next hdc, (hdc in next 2 hdc, work FPdc around next hdc) across to last hdc, hdc in last hdc.

Note: Loop a short piece of thread around any stitch to mark Row 2 as **right** side.

Row 3: Ch 1, turn; hdc in first hdc, work BPdc around next st, (hdc in next 2 hdc, work BPdc around next st) across to last hdc, hdc in last hdc.

Row 4: Ch 1, turn; hdc in first hdc, work FPdc around next st, (hdc in next 2 hdc, work FPdc around next st) across to last hdc, hdc in last hdc.

Rows 5-34: Repeat Rows 3 and 4, 15 times.

Rows 35 and 36: Ch 1, turn; sc in each st across.

Row 37 (Buttonhole row)**:** Ch 1, turn; sc in first 2 sc, ch 5, ★ skip next 3 sc, sc in next sc, ch 5; repeat from ★ once **more**, skip next 3 sc, sc in last 2 sc; finish off.

BUTTON BAND

Row 1: With **right** side facing and working in free loops of beginning ch ***(Fig. 2, page 29)***, join thread with sc in first ch ***(see Joining With Sc, page 29)***; sc in each ch across: 15 sc.

Rows 2-4: Ch 1, turn; sc in each sc across.

Finish off.

FIRST RUFFLE

Row 1: With **right** side facing and working across length of Body, join thread with sc around first FPdc on Row 34; ★ ch 5, skip BPdc on next row, sc around FPdc on next row; repeat from ★ across: 16 ch-5 sps.

Row 2: Ch 1, turn; (sc, hdc) in first ch-5 sp, ch 2, ★ (hdc, dc, work Picot, tr) in next ch-5 sp; repeat from ★ across to last ch-5 sp, (hdc, sc, slip st) in last ch-5 sp; finish off.

SECOND THROUGH FIFTH RUFFLES

With **right** side facing and joining thread with sc around next FPdc on Row 34, work same as First Ruffle.

EDGING

With **wrong** side facing and working in ends of rows, join thread with sc in first row; (ch 5, skip next row, sc in next row) across; finish off: 20 ch-5 sps.

Repeat on opposite edge.

Last Row: With **right** side facing and working across long edge, join thread with sc in first ch-5 sp at Button Band end; hdc in same sp, ch 2, † (hdc, dc, work Picot, tr) in next ch-5 sp and in each ch-5 sp across to last ch-5 sp, (hdc, sc) in last ch-5 sp †, ch 1; working in sc and ch-5 sps across Row 37; sc in first 2 sc, (2 sc, ch 2, 2 sc) in each of next 3 ch-5 sps, sc in last 2 sc, ch 1; working across long edge, (sc, hdc) in next ch-5 sp, repeat from † to † once; finish off.

Sew buttons to Button Band opposite buttonholes.

Cameo Bracelet

EASY +

Approximate Finished Size: $^{7}/_{8}$" wide" x 7½" long (22 mm x 19 cm) (excluding clasp)

SHOPPING LIST

Thread (Lace Weight) LACE 0

[350 yards (320 meters) per ball]:

☐ 15 yards (13.5 meters)

Steel Crochet Hook

☐ Size 7 (1.65 mm)

Additional Supplies

☐ Flexible wire beading needle

☐ Silver-tone toggle clasp

☐ 14 mm flat oval stone beads - 5

GAUGE INFORMATION

Each Motif = approximately 1¼" long x $^{7}/_{8}$" wide (3.25 cm x 22 mm)

Gauge is not of great importance; use any size steel crochet hook needed to achieve desired look.

STITCH GUIDE

TREBLE CROCHET ***(abbreviated tr)***

YO twice, insert hook in sp indicated, YO and pull up a loop (4 loops on hook), (YO and draw through 2 loops on hook) 3 times.

MOTIF (Make 5)

Leaving a long end for sewing, ch 6; join with slip st to form a ring.

Rnd 1 (Right side)**:** Ch 1, (5 hdc, dc, tr, dc) in ring twice; join with slip st to first hdc: 10 hdc, 4 dc, and 2 tr.

Note: Loop a short piece of thread around any stitch to mark Rnd 1 as **right** side.

Rnd 2: Ch 1, sc in same st as joining and in next 5 sts, 3 hdc in next tr, sc in next 7 sts, 3 hdc in next tr, sc in last dc; join with slip st to first sc: 20 sts.

Rnd 3: ★ (Ch 3, dc) in same st, skip next st, slip st in next st; repeat from ★ around, ending by working last slip st in same st as joining slip st, finish off.

FINISHING

See Finishing, pages 30 and 31.

Using photo as a guide for placement and long ends, sew one bead to **right** side of each Motif.

Sew Motifs together, working through third ch of ch-3 at ends of Motifs, forming a strip. Sew half of toggle clasp to each end.

Blue Diamonds Bracelet & Earrings Set

EASY +

Approximate Finished Sizes: Bracelet: 7/8" wide x 7" long (22 mm x 18 cm) (including clasp)
Earring: 2" (5 cm) long (excluding ear wire)

SHOPPING LIST

Thread (Lace Weight) LACE 0

[350 yards (320 meters) per ball]:

- ☐ 15 yards (13.5 meters)

Steel Crochet Hook

- ☐ Size 7 (1.65 mm)

Additional Supplies

- ☐ Silver-tone 2" (5 cm) head pins - 5
- ☐ Toggle clasp
- ☐ Silver-tone fishhook ear wires - 2
- ☐ Silver-tone 6 mm bead caps - 7
- ☐ 6 mm round stone beads - 5
- ☐ 8 mm glass faceted beads - 5
- ☐ Silver-tone 6 mm beads - 4
- ☐ Round-nose pliers - 1 pair
- ☐ Chain-nose pliers - 2 pair
- ☐ Wire cutters

GAUGE INFORMATION

Each Motif (from point to point) =
approximately $^{7}/_{8}$" (22 mm)

Gauge is not of great importance; use any size steel crochet hook needed to achieve desired look.

STITCH GUIDE

FRONT POST DOUBLE CROCHET *(abbreviated FPdc)*

YO, insert hook from **front** to **back** around post of dc indicated ***(Fig. 3, page 29)***, YO and pull up a loop even with last st made (3 loops on hook), (YO and draw through 2 loops on hook) twice.

MOTIF (Make 6)

Rnd 1 (Right side)**:** Using an adjustable ring ***(Figs. 1a-d, page 29)***, ch 2 **(does not count as a st)**, (dc, ch 2) 4 times in ring; join with slip st to first dc: 4 dc and 4 ch-2 sps.

Rnd 2: Ch 1, sc in same st as joining, (sc, ch 1, sc) in next ch-2 sp, ★ sc in next dc, (sc, ch 1, sc) in next ch-2 sp; repeat from ★ 2 times **more**; join with slip st to first sc: 12 sc and 4 ch-1 sps.

Rnd 3: Ch 1, sc in same st as joining, work FPdc around first dc on Rnd 1, ch 2, slip st in top of FPdc just made, sc in in next sc, (sc, ch 2, sc) in next ch-1 sp, ★ sc in next sc, work FPdc around next dc on Rnd 1, ch 2, slip st in top of FPdc just made, sc in next sc, (sc, ch 2, sc) in next ch-1 sp; repeat ★ 2 times **more**; join with slip st to first sc, finish off.

FINISHING

See Finishing, pages 30 and 31.

EARRING (Make 2)
Make bead drop, placing one bead cap and one 6 mm round stone bead on head pin. Using chain-nose pliers, open loop.

Insert loop in any ch-1 sp on one Motif and close loop with pliers.

Using remaining length of head pin, make a loop, inserting it in ch-1 sp on opposite side of same Motif; close this new loop with pliers.

Place one 8 mm bead and one silver-tone bead on head pin, then trim end to ½" (12 mm) if needed. Make a loop, inserting it through fishhook ear wire and close loop with pliers.

Repeat for second Earring.

BRACELET
Make 2 bead drops by placing 8 mm beads on head pins, trimming ends to ½" (12 mm) and making loops to attach. Make one bead drop, placing one bead cap and a 6 mm stone bead on a head pin, trimming end to ½" (12 mm) and making a loop to attach.

Using remaining lengths of head pins in same manner as Earrings, trimming ends to ½" (12 mm) if needed and making loops at each end to attach, assemble Bracelet as follows:

Attach one loop of first head pin in loop at end of toggle clasp, placing one silver-tone bead on opposite end, then attach same head pin in any ch-1 sp on one Motif.
† Attach one loop of next head pin in ch-1 sp on opposite side of **same** Motif. Place a bead cap, a 6 mm round stone bead, and a bead cap on opposite end, then attach same head pin to any ch-1 sp on next Motif.
Attach one loop of next head pin in ch-1 sp on opposite side of **same** Motif †, placing an 8 mm bead on opposite end, then attach same head pin in any ch-1 sp on next Motif. Repeat from † to † once; place a silver-tone bead on opposite end of last head pin and attach same head pin to remaining end of toggle clasp.
Using photo as a guide for placement, open loops on bead drops and attach one 8 mm bead drop to each 6 mm round stone bead loop and one 6 mm round stone bead drop to 8 mm bead loop.

Charming Braid Necklace

Approximate Finished Size: ½" wide x 15" long (12 mm x 38 cm) (including clasp)

EASY +

SHOPPING LIST

Thread (Lace Weight) LACE 0

[721 yards (660 meters) per ball**]**:
- ☐ 100 yards (91 meters)

Steel Crochet Hook
- ☐ Size 7 (1.65 mm)

Additional Supplies
- ☐ Tapestry needle
- ☐ 2" (5 cm) brass head pins - 6
- ☐ Brass toggle clasp
- ☐ 7/8" (22 mm) wire-wrapped brass ring
- ☐ Brass chain with ¼" (7 mm) links - 4 links
- ☐ 6 mm faceted stone bead
- ☐ 12 mm pearl
- ☐ 3 mm beads - 2
- ☐ Metallic cylinder beads - 2
- ☐ Round-nose pliers - 1 pair
- ☐ Chain-nose pliers - 2 pair
- ☐ Wire cutters

GAUGE INFORMATION

Braid (before braiding) =
approximately 1½" (3.75 cm) wide
Gauge is not of great importance; use any size steel crochet hook needed to achieve desired look.

BRAID (Make 2)

Leaving a long end for sewing, ch 16.

Row 1 (Right side)**:** Hdc in second ch from hook and in each ch across: 15 hdc.

Note: Loop a short piece of thread around any stitch to mark Row 1 as **right** side and bottom edge.

Row 2: Ch 15, turn; skip first 14 hdc, slip st in last hdc: 15 chs.

Row 3: Ch 1, turn; hdc in each ch across: one chain loop made.

Rows 4-49: Repeat Rows 2 and 3, 23 times: 24 chain loops made.

Finish off.

FINISHING

See Finishing, pages 30 and 31.

Thread tapestry needle with long end. With **right** side facing, sew chains at base of first and last hdc on Row 1 together to form a chain loop, do **not** cut thread.

With **right** side facing and starting at bottom edge, pull second chain loop from **wrong** side to **right** side through the first loop, then pull the third chain loop through the second chain loop, etc., until all chain loops have been used.

Using same long end, sew toggle clasp to bottom edge.

Repeat with remaining Braid.

Sew last chain loop on each Braid to metal ring.

Using head pins and beads, make 6 bead drops.

Attach the pearl bead drop, one 3 mm bead drop, and one cylinder bead drop to end link of brass chain, closing loops with chain-nose pliers.

Attach the 6 mm faceted bead drop and last 3 mm bead drop to next link in same manner.

Skip next link and attach last cylinder bead drop to last link in same manner.

Open skipped link on chain using chain-nose pliers and attach to metal ring.

General Instructions

ABBREVIATIONS

BPdc	Back Post double crochet(s)
ch(s)	chain(s)
cm	centimeters
dc	double crochet(s)
dtr	double treble crochet(s)
FPdc	Front Post double crochet(s)
hdc	half double crochet(s)
mm	millimeters
Rnd(s)	Round(s)
sc	single crochet(s)
sp(s)	space(s)
st(s)	stitch(es)
tr	treble crochet(s)
tr2tog	treble crochet 2 together
YO	yarn over

SYMBOLS & TERMS

★ — work instructions following ★ as many **more** times as indicated in addition to the first time.

† to † — work all instructions from first † to second † **as many** times as specified.

( ) or [ ] — work enclosed instructions **as many** times as specified by the number immediately following **or** work all enclosed instructions in the stitch or space indicated **or** contains explanatory remarks.

colon (:) — the number(s) given after a colon at the end of a row or round denote(s) the number of stitches or spaces you should have on that row or round.

GAUGE

With the exception of the Choker and the Cuff Bracelet, gauge is not of great importance; your projects may be a little larger or smaller without changing the overall effect. For the Choker and the Cuff Bracelet, exact gauge is **essential** for proper fit. Before beginning your project, make the sample swatch given in the individual instructions in the thread and hook specified. After completing the swatch, measure it, counting your stitches and rows carefully. If your swatch is larger or smaller than specified, **make another, changing hook size to get the correct gauge.** Keep trying until you find the size hook that will give you the specified gauge.

Yarn Weight Symbol & Names	LACE 0	SUPER FINE 1	FINE 2	LIGHT 3	MEDIUM 4	BULKY 5	SUPER BULKY 6	JUMBO 7
Type of Yarns in Category	Fingering, size 10 crochet thread	Sock, Fingering, Baby	Sport, Baby	DK, Light Worsted	Worsted, Afghan, Aran	Chunky, Craft, Rug	Super Bulky, Roving	Jumbo, Roving
Crochet Gauge* Ranges in Single Crochet to 4" (10 cm)	32-42 sts**	21-32 sts	16-20 sts	12-17 sts	11-14 sts	8-11 sts	6-9 sts	5 sts and fewer
Advised Hook Size Range	Steel*** 6 to 8, Regular hook B-1	B-1 to E-4	E-4 to 7	7 to I-9	I-9 to K-10½	K-10½ to M/N-13	M/N-13 to Q	Q and larger

*GUIDELINES ONLY: The chart above reflects the most commonly used gauges and hook sizes for specific yarn categories.

** Lace weight yarns are usually crocheted with larger hooks to create lacy openwork patterns. Accordingly, a gauge range is difficult to determine. Always follow the gauge stated in your pattern.

*** Steel crochet hooks are sized differently from regular hooks–the higher the number, the smaller the hook, which is the reverse of regular hook sizing.

CROCHET TERMINOLOGY		
UNITED STATES		INTERNATIONAL
slip stitch (slip st)	=	single crochet (sc)
single crochet (sc)	=	double crochet (dc)
half double crochet (hdc)	=	half treble crochet (htr)
double crochet (dc)	=	treble crochet (tr)
treble crochet (tr)	=	double treble crochet (dtr)
double treble crochet (dtr)	=	triple treble crochet (ttr)
triple treble crochet (tr tr)	=	quadruple treble crochet (qtr)
skip	=	miss

STEEL CROCHET HOOKS																
U.S.	00	0	1	2	3	4	5	6	7	8	9	10	11	12	13	14
Metric - mm	3.5	3.25	2.75	2.25	2.1	2	1.9	1.8	1.65	1.5	1.4	1.3	1.1	1	.85	.75

JOINING WITH SC

When instructed to join with sc, begin with a slip knot on hook. Insert hook in stitch or space indicated, YO and pull up a loop, YO and draw through both loops on hook.

ADJUSTABLE LOOP

Wind yarn around two fingers to form a ring ***(Fig. 1a)***. Slide yarn off fingers and grasp the strands at the top of the ring ***(Fig. 1b)***. Insert hook from **front** to **back** into the ring, pull up a loop, YO and draw through loop on hook to lock ring ***(Fig. 1c)*** (st made does **not** count as part of beginning ch of first rnd). Working around **both** strands, follow instructions to work sts in the ring, then pull yarn tail to close ***(Fig. 1d)***.

Fig. 1a

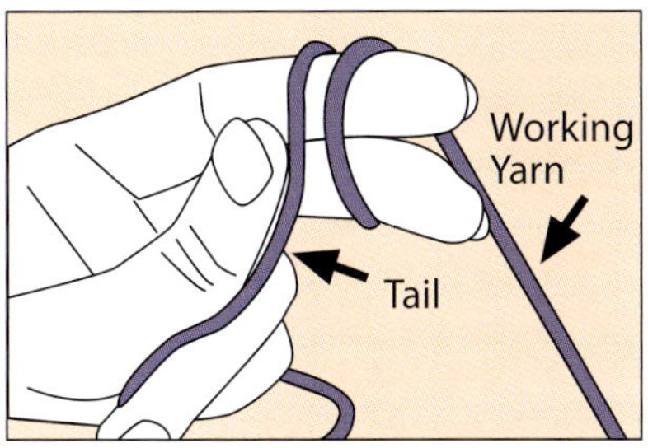

Fig. 1b

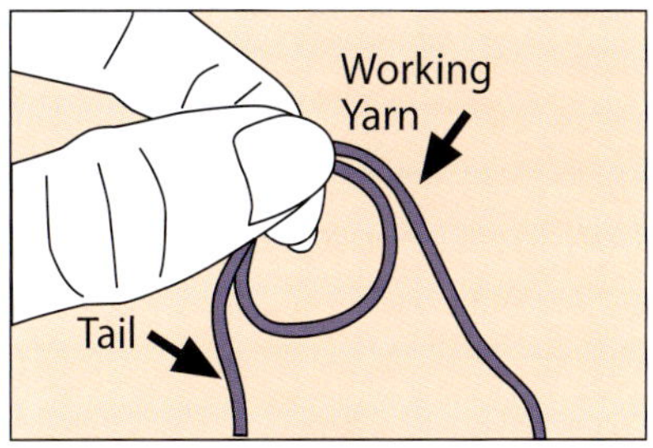

Fig. 1c

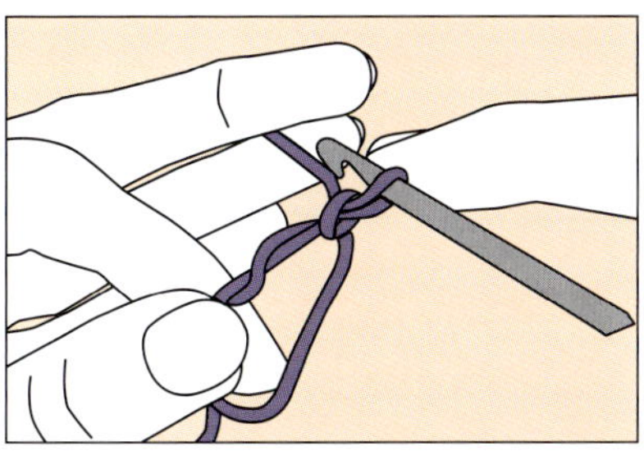

Fig. 1d

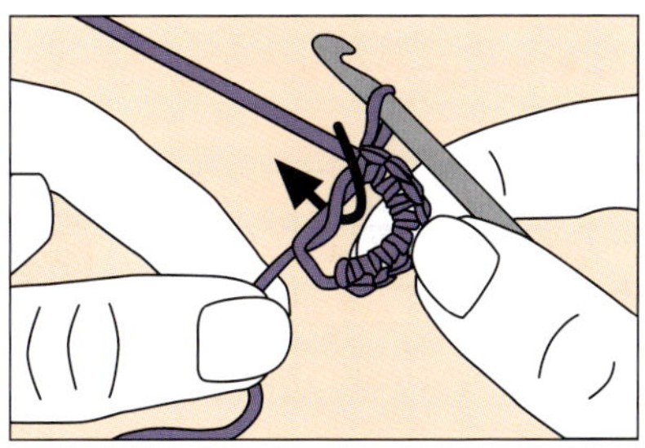

FREE LOOPS OF A CHAIN

When instructed to work in free loops of a chain, work in loop indicated by arrow ***(Fig. 2)***.

Fig. 2

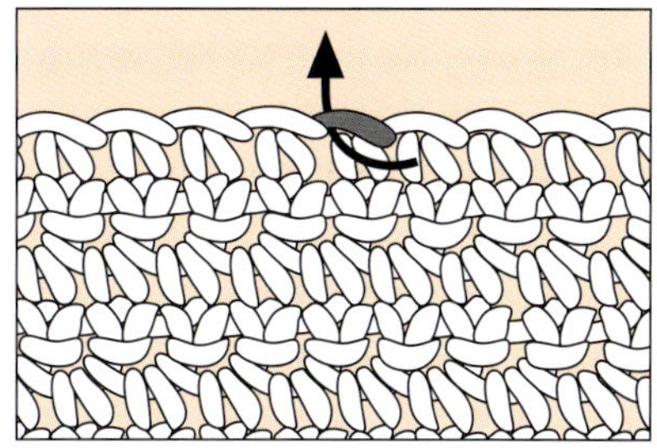

POST STITCH

Work around post of stitch indicated, inserting hook in direction of arrow ***(Fig. 3)***.

Fig. 3

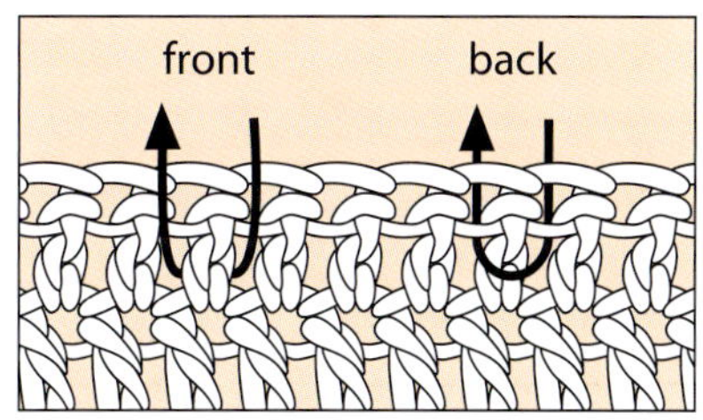

BEGINNER	Projects for first-time crocheters using basic stitches. Minimal shaping.
EASY	Projects using yarn with basic stitches, repetitive stitch patterns, simple color changes, and simple shaping and finishing.
INTERMEDIATE	Projects using a variety of techniques, such as basic lace patterns or color patterns, mid-level shaping and finishing.
EXPERIENCED	Projects with intricate stitch patterns, techniques and dimension, such as non-repeating patterns, multi-color techniques, fine threads, small hooks, detailed shaping and refined finishing.

FINISHING COMPONENTS

All components used in this book can be found in the beading/jewelry section of any craft store. Here are products similar to the ones we used.

Bails are attached to beads and other objects to create pendants. They come in many sizes, shapes, and designs.

Bead caps add texture and sparkle when placed next to beads.

Chains come in a veriety of sizes, styles, color, and finishes.

Chandelier findings provide a base with bottom loops to which bead drops and other embellishments can be attached and a top loop for attaching an ear wire.

Clasps of all sizes, shapes, and styles are available. **Lobster clasps** are shaped like a lobster's claw and have a spring-action closure. A **toggle clasp** is secured by sliding the bar through the loop.

Just about any earring style can be made with the wide variety of **ear wires** available — fishhook and lever-back are used in this book.

A **head pin** is straight wire with a head of some sort; the ones used in this book are flat but there are several decorative styles as well.

Jump rings are metal round or oval rimgs that are used to attach jewelry components to each other. The rings are opened and closed with chain-nose pliers.

Bails

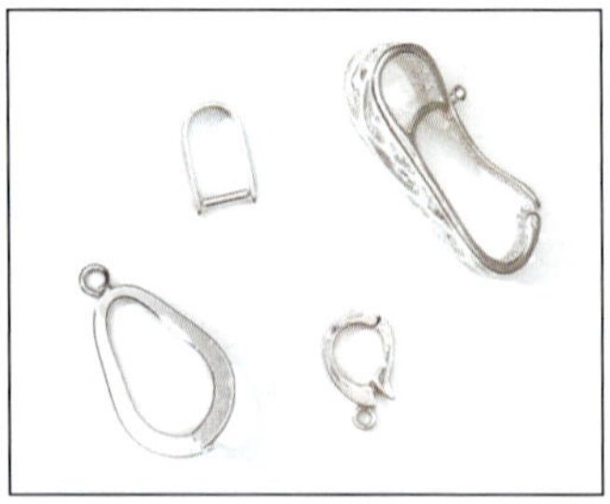

Chains

Lobster Clasps

Fishhook Ear Wires

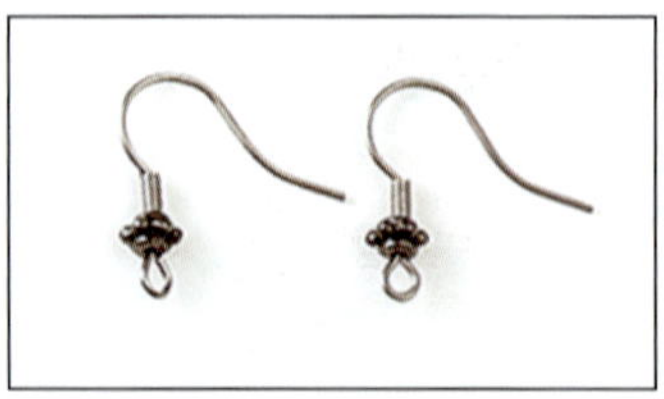

Jump Rings

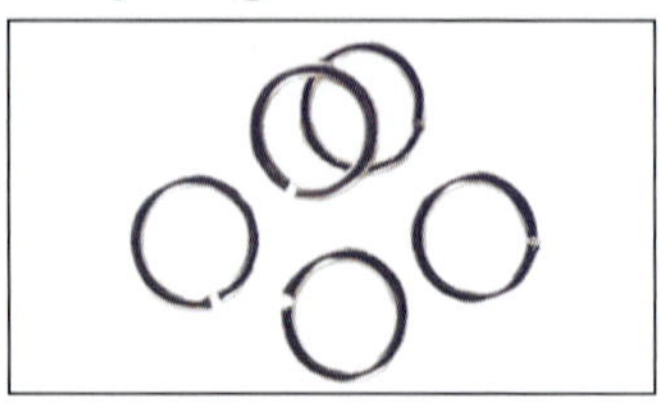

Bead Caps

Chandelier findings

Toggle Clasps

Lever-back Ear Wires

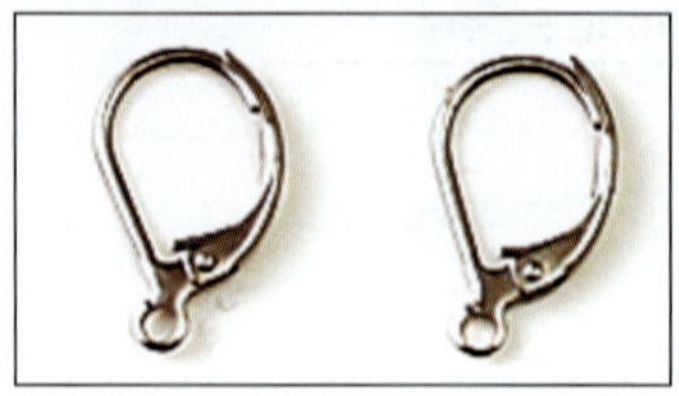

Head Pins

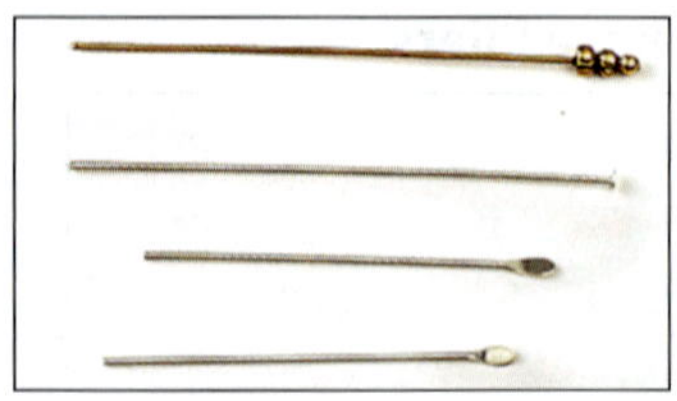

TOOLS

Chain-nose pliers have rounded, tapered jaws and a flat interior that will not mar wire or metal findings. These pliers are used for opening and closing jump rings and bending wire. You will need 2 pair to open jump rings and loops on head pins and ear wires.

Round-nose pliers have round jaws that are useful for making loops and bending wire smoothly.

Wire cutters are used to cut beading wire, head pins and other soft metals.

A **flexible wire beading needle** has a collapsible eye that allows it to go through small-hole beads and can be used to sew Motifs together.

Chain-nose Pliers

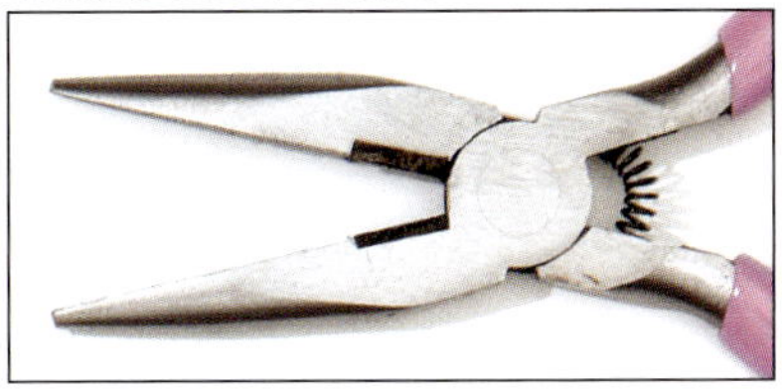

Round-nose Pliers

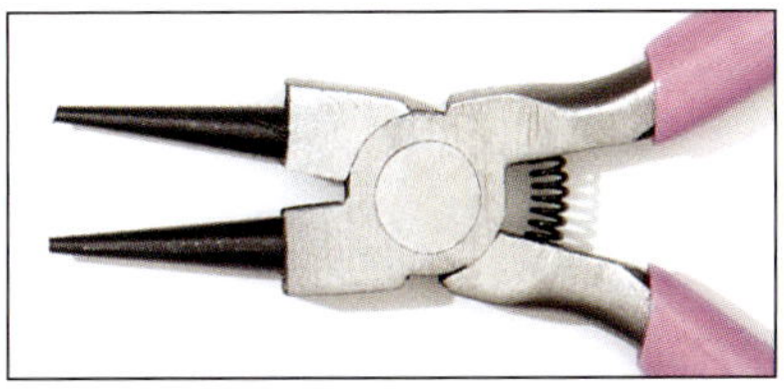

Wire Cutters

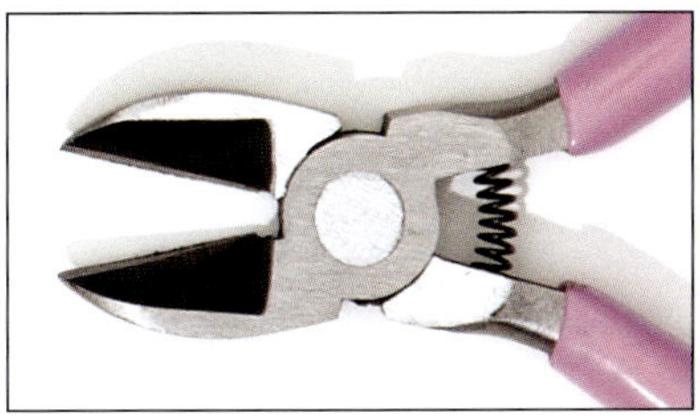

Wire Beading Needle

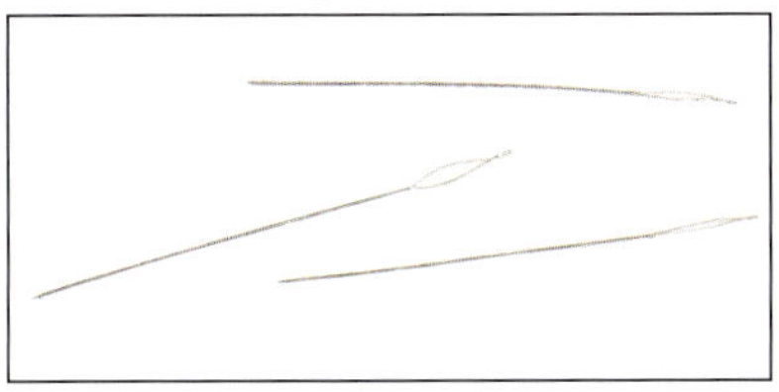

MAKING BEAD DROPS ON HEAD PINS

Slide bead on your head pin. Leaving about ½" (12 mm), cut off excess wire. Using the chain-nose pliers, bend the wire at a 90° angle ***(Fig. 4a)***. Grasp the wire end with the round-nose pliers. Turn the pliers and bend the wire into a loop ***(Figs. 4b & c)***. Release the pliers. Straighten or twist the loop further if necessary.

Fig. 4a

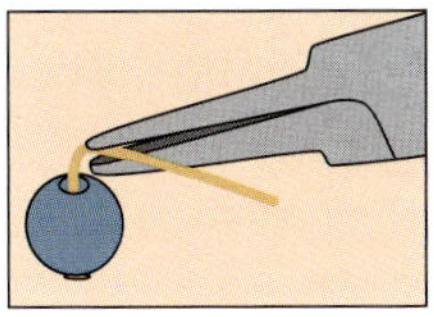

Fig. 4b

Fig. 4c

OPENING AND CLOSING JUMP RINGS AND LOOPS

Pick up a jump ring with chain-nose pliers. With a second pair of chain-nose pliers, gently hold the other side of the ring. Open the ring by pulling one pair of pliers toward you while pushing the other away ***(Fig. 5)***.

Fig. 5

Close the ring by pushing and pulling the pliers in the opposite direction, bringing the ring ends together.

You will also open and close the loops on head pins and ear wires the same way.

Meet Kristen Stoltzfus Clay

Heavily influenced by her love for vintage and retro designs, Kristen Stoltzfus Clay began freelance crochet designing in 2010 at age 19, after years of adapting or making up patterns for her own needs. "My first sold design was a thread jewelry design, and I've never lost that love," she said.

Kristen is recently married and starting a family with her husband on his five-generation ranch in rural Idaho. "I'm blessed to be living my dream every day," she said. "I also am deeply interested in vintage fashion and sewing, enjoy cooking from scratch and other old-fashioned ways of life, antiquing, old movies and music, history, writing, exploring Idaho, and watching the beautiful hills change color every evening."

For more about Kristen, visit her Etsy shop, Joys in Stitches, or her blog at verityvintagestudio.typepad.com.

Thread Information

Each item in this book was made using Lace Weight cotton thread, also known as bedspread weight, size 10. Any brand of Lace Weight cotton thread may be used. Remember, to arrive at the finished size, it is the GAUGE/TENSION that is important, not the brand of thread.

For your convenience, listed below are the specific threads used to create our photography models. Because thread manufacturers make frequent changes to their product lines, you may sometimes find it necessary to use a substitute thread or to search for the discontinued product at alternate suppliers (locally or online).

FILIGREE PENDANT
Knit Picks® Curio
#26269 Spearmint

HIBISCUS NECKLACE
Knit Picks® Curio
#26270 Victorian

ALL KEYED UP NECKLACE
Knit Picks® Curio
#26264 Comfrey

OLIVE EARRINGS
Aunt Lydia's® Classic 10™
#672 Olive

RING TIME NECKLACE & EARRINGS SET
Handy Hands Lizbeth®
#644 Dk Boysenberry

FLOWER BROOCH
Aunt Lydia's® Classic 10™
White - #1 White
Cream - #420 Cream

CHOKER & EARRINGS SET
Universal Yarn® Nazli Gelin® Garden
#700-09

STAR FLOWER EARRINGS
Version A
Aunt Lydia's® Classic 10™
#661 Frosty Green
Version B
Knit Picks® Curio
#26259 Hollyberry

RUFFLED CUFF BRACELET
Aunt Lydia's® Classic 10™
#210 Antique White

CAMEO BRACELET
Aunt Lydia's® Classic 10™
#435 Silver

BLUE DIAMONDS BRACELET & EARRINGS SET
Aunt Lydia's® Classic 10™
#480 Delft

CHARMING BRAID NECKLACE
Knit Picks® Curio
#26268 Ciel

We have made every effort to ensure that these instructions are accurate and complete. We cannot, however, be responsible for human error, typographical mistakes, or variations in individual work.

Production Team: Writer/Instructional Editor - Sarah J. Green; Editorial Writer - Susan Frantz Wiles; Senior Graphic Artist - Lora Puls; Graphic Artist - Kellie McAnulty; Photo Stylist - Lori Wenger; and Photographer - Jason Masters.

Made in U.S.A.